W9-ACJ-050

Everything Winged Must Be Dreaming

EVERYTHING

WINGED

MUST BE

DREAMING

POEMS BY

SUSAN LUDVIGSON

LOUISIANA STATE UNIVERSITY PRESS

BATON ROUGE AND LONDON 1993

Manufactured in the United States of America
First printing
02 01 00 99 98 97 96 95 94 93   5 4 3 2 1
Designer: Amanda McDonald Key
Typeface: Sabon
Typesetter: Precision Typographers, Inc.
Printer and binder: Thomson–Shore, Inc.

Library of Congress Cataloging-in-Publication Data

Ludvigson, Susan.
    Everything winged must be dreaming : poems / by Susan Ludvigson.
        p.   cm.
    ISBN 0-8071-1836-2. — ISBN 0-8071-1837-0 (pbk.)
    I. Title.
    PS3562.U27E9   1993   93-10738
    811'.54—dc20   CIP

The author offers grateful acknowledgment to the editors of the
publications in which the following poems first appeared: "The
Visitation," *American Voice* (Spring, 1992); "The Difficult Life of Ideas,"
Chariton Review, XVII (Spring, 1991); "Sfumato," *Contents,* No. 6
(1993); "Rainy Morning in Puivert," *Georgia Review,* XLVI (Spring,
1992); "It Begins with a Presentiment," *Georgia Review,* XLVII (Summer,
1993); "After Love," *Kansas Quarterly* (1993); "The Pal Lunch," *Kenyon
Review,* XIV (Summer, 1992); "How Seem Bedeviled Be," *Michigan
Quarterly Review,* XXXII (Spring, 1993); "Gabriel's Story," *Mississippi
Review,* XX, No. 2 (Spring, 1992); "The Owl Snake," *Mississippi Review,*
XX, No. 3 (Spring, 1992); "What If," *Nation* (November 23, 1992);
"Poem to the Ideal Reader" and "Rehearsals," *New Virginia Review*
(Summer, 1993); "Grace," *Ohio Review* No. 48 (1992); "In a Difficult
Key" and "Roses," *Pendragon,* XI (1993); "Blackberries" and "Lasting,"
Ploughshares, XIX (Spring, 1993); "Happiness: The Forbidden Subject"
and "New Orleans Feather Sculptor Dies of Knife Wounds," *Poetry,* CLVII
(January, 1991); "The Map of Imagined Geography," *Shenandoah,* XLIII
(Spring, 1993); "October in the Aude," *Snail's Pace Review,* I (Spring,
1991); "This Ordinary Waltz" and "Visiting Einstein in Washington,
D.C.," *Southern California Anthology,* No. 11 (1993); "Dreaming
Another Version," *Southern Humanities Review,* XXVII (Fall, 1993);
"*Etiam Peccata,*" *Southern Poetry Review,* XXXII (Fall, 1992); "Inventing
My Parents" and "Watching Myself Compose," *Southern Review,* XXVIII
(Autumn, 1992); "Containing the Light" and "*Monde Renversé,*" *Tar
River Poetry,* XXXIII (1993); "Sophie's Father Visits" and "Jasmine,"
Yemassee, I (Spring, 1993); "Blackberries" published in 1993 by Duende
Press; "Sophie's Father Visits" published in an anthology edited by Stephen
Corey.

The author would like to thank the Rockefeller Foundation for a
fellowship to the Bellagio Center in Italy, where a number of these poems
were written.

For Scott

CONTENTS

EVERYTHING WINGED MUST BE DREAMING

THE MAP OF IMAGINED GEOGRAPHY

For Stephen Hall

One 16th century map of the world
is remarkably accurate,
latitude and longitude somehow
divined, the cartographer inspired,
like a blind man who feels his way
through any universe, outlines of ideas
imprinted in his fingertips. Angel faces
blow the winds of the world from the margins,
three dark mouths from the south, nine
white ones, lips puckered as for kisses,
warm breath, cold breath, puffs
of cumulus clouds surrounding each
disembodied head. Australia is a vacancy
smooth as drugged sleep,
and North America blurs to a dream.

In the Bar Rossi this morning
a man tells me he nearly died on Friday,
his car a tangle of steel and blood.
His mother weeps. His father
shakes his head, orders cappuccino
for celebration. A dark-eyed woman,
their friend, translates the contours
of two Italian lakes, and the way streets
intersect the town, into slow words
they think they can follow. The man
who feels resurrected, whose face
is swollen, bruised, remembers
nothing of his trajectory,
only light smashing into his eyes
like something he might have seen
in a movie, and an explosion
of sound he thought was his soul.
He could not trace
his way back to the road
but envisions the region as time
when absence filled him like the freezing
lake, a silver territory his mind

swam in, arms flailing, eyes open,
seeing nothing. He emerged
two days ago after wandering the depths
where invisible mountains
rise and shift and change, by stages,
the visible world. On another map
they'd be radiant red patches lifting
toward the surface while iridescent blues
at the edges sink, the earth's floor
dropping and dropping. Today,
dawn arrives from the definition
of the valley where he's learned
to look for it, where it will be tomorrow.

RAINY MORNING IN PUIVERT

The sky as thunder rattles the distance
is a blue that, were it paint
on canvas, would be garish, a teal fog
obscuring the Pyrenees, whose hazy
outline can scarcely be seen,
like a dream you're calling
into consciousness.

Our neighbor, Odette, recently widowed,
fears thunderstorms. She keeps
shutters closed on a day like this,
wanders from one small room to another
thinking of Paul. Too early for me
to go over, and by the time
it's a proper hour, rain will slash
across the road. Is this an excuse?

I love lightning from enough distance,
the whole sky brilliantly open
and then dissolving darkly
back into itself, like something human,
a love affair, then love gone wrong.

"Married over fifty years," she said.
That's our goal. To wake together,
some part of one body touching
the other, listening to rain
on a tile roof, the faint fragrance
of woodsmoke.

No reason to go out.
Everything's closed on Mondays.
I'll watch the sky gradually change,
the Cathar chateau's ruined tower
emerge from mist the way history
asserts itself here—
insistent as all beauty.

Only Lascale, a smaller village
up the road, wants to let the past go.
Burned by the Germans, everyone killed,
now its symmetrical new tile look
could be any suburb of Carcassonne.

Here, everything's old. This tiny house
had a huge carved stone set into a wall.
From when the chateau began to crumble,
late 15th century? Nobody knows.
There's a shape on the left
like a Celtic clover, on the right,
a sand dollar figure, a small
heart above, the whole encased
in a large one. The world's heaviest
valentine, we joke. We had it removed
from its hidden corner to rest
on the wide pine boards
in front of the bed. Perhaps it was
a marriage gift, someone said—
two symbols the crests of families,
the heart above and the heart around
meanings that never alter.
So *logique* we believe it.
And want to. We started
our marriage here, two years ago.

The rain has stopped.
A white cloud rises so fast
in the distance, I think of the bomb.
But of course not. Already
it diffuses, is shaped by a subtle
wind, ascends, begins to join
the pale clean sky
swallows are circling again.

HOW SEEM BEDEVILED BE

On the marriage of Elsie and Wallace Stevens

She was Bo-Peep, bedazzling him
with eyelet pinafores
and almond petit-fours.

Be ribboned, he said, let daisies
undulate through your yellow hair
like the hair Yeats claimed

was reason enough for reason
to fly. Blond curls,
billowing, bound him,

gold threads wound
round his heart like braid.
She half-believed, and the letters

rained. They spilled through the roof
of Reading nights, words
slipping their wet way

into her bed,
so that her sleep rolled
with sounds still round

on her tongue as they came
from him. And there were
rainbows on her skin.

The indigo of incidents he sent
was lavender to her loneliness.
She walked the days away,

her adopted name away, on paths
he said were bent to fit
her silken feet, poor indolent Peep.

Poor Princess.
Her nights were a cathedral built
to hold the soul he thought

was his, wrought a different
way, perhaps, but sister somehow
to his own. Hardly a kiss

had passed their lips, an occasional
dove, its feathers brushing
sweet as a breeze fresh

from the lush printemps.
She teased, and he,
tentative, testy, whispered

of cleaving, chastity, chill.
On the porch swing, under
her mother's nervous eye—

the knowing, unhaphazard eye
she cast on preachers,
poachers, pillars

of the community, they rocked,
she sang a lullaby.
Years passed like this, in sometime

bliss. But mostly she grew tired.
The words got thin as autumn grass,
the months rolled on in carriages

whose passengers they rarely were.
Patience, he said, was the fullest
word, the plumpest bird to watch

display its plumage—slow—
an opening that the peacock knew
and he had come to know.

When the woods came white again
the fifth time round, he gave
his pledge. A secret to be closeted

'til pink proclaimed ascendency
(the secret, of course,
from his family).

The choirs didn't sing the solemn day
he carried her over the estuary
into summer. She feared her voice

might never touch that inner string
he plucked himself, to set
his spirit humming.

What if she'd found another man,
a simpler friend, a lover
who would look at a sea and see a sea,

who'd have looked at her and seen Elsie—
no angel of necessity
or figment of reality.

She might have found fair words herself.
Might have turned the burnished sky
into a sign of ecstasy, might have

allowed her mind to glide
into the embrace of buoys
drifting in Miami's bay.

Instead, the giant settled her
in a silent house, saving words
for the prayers

he made—and only made—on paper.
Oh, it was a silvery cage,
to be sure and sure.

Then he became the mountain king,
and on certain nights of their middle age,
an alabaster avalanche.

She was the rock he fell against.

AFTER LOVE

She remembers how reason
escaped from the body,
flew out with a sigh,
went winging up
to a corner of the ceiling
and fluttered there,
a moth, a translucence,
waiting.

She did not hear it
return, did not see
but felt its brush
against her breasts
quieter, quieter,
until it slipped
back in, powdered
wings intact.

ETIAM PECCATA

For Carol Pharr

On the liaison of Roza Scribor-Rylska and Paul Claudel

In my arms I have held the human star.
— Paul Claudel, "L'Esprit et l'Eau"

OCTOBER, 1900
He falls even faster
than I do, so that when we're both
underwater, he looks surprised,
those great blue eyes open, blinking,
while I dive between his legs,
mermaid, fish, and grasp him
by the waist. Then he's there,
he's with me, and it's
as if there were no husband, sons,
calling from shore in voices
too muffled to hear. We twist
and turn under the waves,
lightning zigzagging
tumultuous water.
We're a ballet, attuned
as mirror images,
blond hair swirling round our heads.
Haloes, Paul says through bubbles,
laughing.

1901
Rosalie, he says. Rosalia, Rosa,
moj kotku, my kitten.
Roza's my name. But I'll be
his Rosalie here, anywhere.
China's so vast, we can be lost
together. Even in Foutcheau—
so many golden rooms in the Consulat,
when the children call from their sleep
I can't hear them. Rosa, he says,
taking my breast in his mouth,
my breasts still full, not
drooping yet from the babies.
White as the sun, he says,

when you look long enough into it,
sun on the ocean's horizon.
Isolde, he says.

1902

In my bed, in my gilded room,
he is the sun and the moon.
I didn't imagine those hands
so capable. You are not handsome,
I said to him once. He laughed,
his hands white birds in the air.
That was before. Now
he doesn't laugh, but slips
them under me, pulls me hard
against him, sometimes weeping.
Your eyes are oceans, I say,
and he doesn't smile,
but closes them, reaches
for me, runs his hands over my body
as if he were searching for something
not there. I turn to those hands.

1903

Sinners, he calls us.
He speaks my husband's name
in the middle of love,
rolls away before the rapture can come
to take us out of ourselves
so that we hover somewhere
above our bodies, the room
insubstantial as air.

I am learning to write
Chinese characters.
The one that means love is too complex,
but here is "to be together, to fit"— 共同一致
and here is "bewitch"— 使着迷
I give them to Paul,
who tells me to learn
the figure for God.
I do— 上帝
He is not satisfied,
not even pleased.

Now when he parts my legs
in the darkness,
I fear for the end.
The sounds escaping from him
are growls, like pain.
He says it's his soul slipping away.

I take my sons out to the garden.
They feed the swallows
that swoop almost into their laps
for the bread.
My sons are like birds themselves,
small-boned like their father.
I think of their father, who chose
the jungle, a dangerous
mission for money,
how he installed me with Paul
and went whistling away.

Paul spends hours in the chapel.
He wants to do penance,
but can't, for I'm in an upstairs
bedroom, humming, and he feels
himself pulled in, he says.
He says I'm making him do this.
I say nothing as he unbuttons
my dress, puts his shaking hands
on my breasts, and pushes me
onto the bed.

1904
What is the soul, I ask him,
that it should make such demands?
Woman, he tells me, you are
the spirit's fever, you raise
the temperature until
it dies, delirious, thirsty.
When I tell him I have fever
myself, he leaves the room.

The Chinese doctor has hands
like a woman's, gentle and lithe
as lilies. I'm pregnant,
he tells us. Paul's face
is porcelain. And then it cracks.

I pack my valises. Trembling
with calm, I tell Paul,
Because you believe you need to choose,
you must choose God. I know
you now. You think your body
is the enemy—and mine. You think
of our flesh as having made pacts,
bargains you can't control.

I'm surprised when he yells at me:
No, it's too late!
He orders the cook to make quail
he'd imported from France,
and brings out one of the hoarded
Saint-Emilions. He laughs,
but the sound is like coughing.
I'm already lost, he says.
Don't go.

But I'm gone. And I take
such a circuitous route,
he can't follow: Japan,
San Francisco, New York.
I'm in Belgium now, where winter
makes hard white tracks
on my heart.
He's learned where I am
and writes letters so fat
I wonder what else he must do
with his days. No need to open
or read them. I know
what they say.

The baby is growing large
inside me, my breasts
meet my belly. I'm carrying
high this time. Can it mean
a girl? A pain begins above
my right hip, moves around
my back to the left, where
it settles drunkenly in,
close to the baby.

JANUARY 22, 1905

It *is* a girl. An easier birth
than the others, easier
than I'd prepared for,
the sheets hardly bloody.
My sister says I'm blessed,
that when the baby came,
her brilliant blue eyes
were already open. Still opaque,
they look like the paper
Paul used to wrap crystal beads—
a gift once, for me.
I'll call her Louise,
after Paul's mother.

APRIL, 1905

My sister warns me
he's coming here.
We pack again, uneasily.
I dream of his weight
the whole length of my body,
dream the moment we'd both
become weightless, the closest
I've been to the flight
of the soul. Blasphemy,
I think sadly.
It's what he'd say.
My arms shiver, even filled
with the warmth of Louise.

I leave a medal of St. Benoit
on the bed for him to find,
an old silver medal
I bought in a shop near here.
I liked the pattern of tarnish,
the saint's eyes dark, staring
into what only he sees.
Poverty. Chastity. Obedience.

SEPTEMBER, 1905

Francis, my husband, is dead.
The telegram came from Cochin China

today. It's what he wanted—to die
with the calls of exotic birds
in his ears.
The boys will be sad, though all
they remember is the day he left them
with kisses and sacks of hard candy.
Am I sad? My heart feels
hollow, as if a man could walk
into it, tap on the walls,
and get nothing but echo.

Paul has learned of my husband's death.
He says now I'll return,
we can marry, can sanctify flesh,
candles filling the chapel,
their smoke carrying sin away.

My answer is No.
He believed his soul was the prize,
that his God and I were engaged
in immortal combat.
Would he marry the devil?

1910
My new husband, whose hair
shines black as a crow's
bright wing under moonlight,
is nothing like Paul.
A good man who thinks
the world is simple, and I
its sapphire center. More babies.
I chose this, I think,
and I choose it each day
I open my eyes
to the velvet drapes
he pulls slowly back
to reveal the room
washed in whiteness.
So why do I weep
at a Chinese teapot
in any store window?
Louise slaps her tiny sister
and I feel my cheek redden.

I flush at a word or a gesture
that's hers, that's her father's.
He's married too. A wife
he let God choose,
and who serves him.

1920

I follow his journeys. I have
fastened a map of America
to my dressing room mirror, and trace
his movements in ink.
His poems are in every
librairie window.
God is his shadow, it seems,
or he the shadow of God
trying to stand in full sunlight.
I buy his books,
their covers plain as a priest's
summer mantle. Each
a reproach.
The poems do not enter me
whole, but in fragments,
like slivers of glass.
When I turn in my sleep
toward my husband,
pain wakes me, pain
not of the flesh, yet rooted
so deep in the body
its source seems everywhere.

1930

It doesn't end.
I dream the sound of his breathing
and wake to his name.
I can hardly pick up *Le Monde*
without seeing that face, grown full,
the photographs always in profile,
so that he seems to be looking
away.

I think of my pride,
how when I left I thought of myself
as a sailboat,

defying the winds,
my small sails filling,
destination unknown.
Now I'm more like a kite
caught in one updraft
after another.
A child, he'd tell me.
You think like a child.
His voice would be rueful,
his mouth trapped
between passion and frown.

1948
The premiere of *Partage de Midi.*
I slip into the Odeon alone,
sit far in the back, discover
his play is our lives, astounding
revision: the carriage of love
rushed him toward Hades
(that much always his truth)
but then—gone—somehow
I became Beatrice,
flicked silver reins, swept
his chariot to heaven.
Transformed to an angel of God,
I was made for one purpose—
to lead him to salvation.

Elixir of lies!

All these years,
in his mind that must carve everything
to a shape that fits squares
like a chessboard
(how could I have forgotten?)
we have been whittled to figures
who move only where he puts them.
I stand, a pawn
in his God's bewildering light,
arms raised in a benediction.
No! I cry into the theater,
my words lost in applause—
I am who I am!

1950
I lead my life. Each Sunday
my children bring their children
to my house. We no longer talk
of the war. When we speak of the past
it's to reminisce—the winter
of no snow, but ice that hung
in intricate constellations
at all the windows,
delicate slips of light
snapping under sun—
or of trips to Spain
when they were young,
.expanses of white sand beach
stretched the length of their memories.

The youngest granddaughter is another
Louise, her hair fair as Paul's,
her frown-wrinkle already his.
I loosen the ribbons in her curls, take her
to the Luxembourg Gardens. Somber,
she pulls her blue boat on the pond
in a single direction, clockwise.
Today, when his name drifts
across the small waves on a wind,
nothing in me takes wing.

SOPHIE'S FATHER VISITS

The sad widower come to spend
some days with her
is not who we'd imagined:
frail, eyes permanently swollen,
his Belgian French making him
cup an ear to understand
the Rumanians and Americans,
whose accents in his language
drift in odd directions,
whose lives are foreign too.
Why did we think he'd be
akin to our neighbors,
whose world is rabbits
and t.v. game shows
and weather falling on us
like a gift or a curse?

He brings out photographs
of his work: *trompe l'oeil*
that makes our hearts repeat
their quick stunned beats.

A wall awash with Sienna
calls us to arched doorways,
umber houses, sun a glaze
over rooftops, sky
the color of dreams.

His *faux marbre* makes me
want to touch what would be cool,
its shining surface veined
and shadowed
where there should be shadow.
We long to lie down on it,
make love there,
where a silver cat
nearly switches its tail.

He makes us think of windows
into gardens
walled and shimmering
with scarlet, bougainvillea
climbing over morning—

a view into the void
imagination turns to paradise.

He walks into a 16th century room,
blank stone plastered white,
walls thick and heavy as grief.
In days a city opens
its shutters, geraniums
leaning out below
a few rapt faces,
rose-skinned women,
chestnut hair
like waterfalls at dusk
flowing past silk shoulders
to pale breasts.

He tells us, now in English,
how at night, after wine,
one can walk with a single candle
into the place the mind makes,
and the hard world dissolves.

INVENTING MY PARENTS

After Edward Hopper's *Nighthawks*, 1942

They sit in the bright cafe
discussing Hemingway, and how
this war will change them.
Sinclair Lewis' name comes up,
and Kay Boyle's, and then Fitzgerald's.
They disagree about the American Dream.
My mother, her bare arms
silver under fluorescent lights,
says she imagines it a hawk
flying over, its shadow sweeping
every town. Their coffee's getting cold
but they hardly notice. My mother's face
is lit by ideas. My father's gestures
are a Frenchman's. When he concedes
a point, he shrugs, an elaborate lift
of the shoulders, his hands and smile
declaring an open mind.

I am five months old, at home with a sitter
this August night, when the air outside
is warm as a bath. They decide,
though the car is parked nearby,
to walk the few blocks home, savoring
the fragrant night, their being alone together.
As they go out the door, he's reciting
Donne's "Canonization": "For God's sake
hold your tongue, and let me love,"
and she's laughing, light
as summer rain when it begins.

HAPPINESS: THE FORBIDDEN SUBJECT

Is it because, longing for it,
so many have ripped up their husbands'
glossy photos, carried their wives'
suitcases to cars, everyone crying
as the Chevrolets and Volkswagens
and Renaults pulled out of driveways?
Because they trained so hard
to climb the pinnacles,
and when they arrived the air
was thinner than they'd imagined,
the views predictable? Or because
they stood in gardens in the dark,
waiting for stars to fall
into their eyes, for new lovers
slimmer than the old,
with voices like the Adriatic
in calm weather? Is it because
they saw it at the ends
of black and white movies, too grainy
to be believed, but they believed,
and remembered Technicolor?
I tell you, we were among them.

So when we found it unexpectedly,
like the bed of four-leafed clover
under the dogwood,
we pronounced its name
with caution. We knew
the history of love,
had seen affection peel
like wallpaper
from our favorite rooms,
the motley patterns behind.

We are so pleased with ourselves,
each other, that we hug the luck
of our bodies every morning,
every night, our prayers
the same each time—
sweet words they'd shake
their heads at, sadly,

muttering, as we would
have muttered once,
of fools who think that life's
a valentine.

GRACE

Walking behind two men, I watch
the long tail of a pheasant drift
and rise, hanging half out
of a pocket made for it, feathers
caught in the small breeze
parting, coming together
like living things. They're September
colors, could make the quills
our neighbor says he'd write with
if he wrote.

The one with the bird has his shotgun
broken, its V slung over his shoulder
an echo of geese. The other
carries his gun in his arms, is calling
the spaniel, who chases a moth
into a ditch.

Dawn again. Sun's a pink slit
between mountains. I wait
for the crack of a shot to slice
the lightening sky. But all the birds
have disappeared—even the swallows
whose spiral above the balcony
at this hour is a mournful concert,
a skittery dance.

Pines in the distance begin to brighten,
deep blue to something like green.

Everything winged must be dreaming.

THE OWL SNAKE

Riding along in the car,
minding our business,
we see at the side of the road
the owl snake slither
out of the woods.
What? I shout, eyeing
its feathery scales, its body
thick with what could almost
be fur. Nothing to worry about,
Scott says. We speed up.
The snake, faster than
horse or train or truck,
is in front of us.
We'll run over him,
Scott says, the car skidding
off to the right, but instead
the snake mounts the hood,
his brushed-brown belly
flattened against the windshield.
I'm screaming.
Don't worry, Scott says,
he can't get in.
But suddenly he's in
my lap, frightened, his head
lifted, swaying like a cobra's
though his tongue's not flicking,
and he's trembling.
Why, I say, he's all right,
he's *nice*. Sure, Scott says.
Then the owl snake begins
to hoot into the night,
and I cradle him in my arms,
his soft fat body relaxing
against me, poor baby.

BLACKBERRIES

Yesterday, picking them again,
again I fell into the brambles,
the ground under me holes and swells
the bushes hid. Socks and jeans
full of stickers, I pulled my scratched
body up and continued plucking, those
berries so plump, so irresistible
I blinked at trickles of blood.
The day before I fell into a ditch
trying to reach across
to the fattest prizes—slipped,
my rump hitting the prickly ground
so hard I thought of sudden love.

The ripest ones
will drop into your hand
at a brush of the branch.
I can spot them now, the ones
so black they're almost blue,
crow colored. That ready,
they don't cling to their pods,
but wish themselves into the air,
onto the tongue.

Today my right hand still burns
from the nettles. The skin seems
to be buzzing—first above the wrist,
then below it, following the pulse.
It makes me dream of blackberries.
I tell you, they ache for pastry
to hold them, for the mouth
I put now to my humming hand.

OCTOBER IN THE AUDE

It comes quickly to the mountains,
changeable winds that carry so many hawks
swooping, circling the same field,
Scott says it's a convention. The same day
we watch a parachute lesson,
a dozen men and women lifting turquoise,
red, fuchsia, brilliant yellow canopies
over their heads as they sprint downhill,
trying to catch a gust, like children
who hope an umbrella will hold them up,
take them over the trees. These silks
are colors you see only in dreams
of impossible flowers,
and they do rise for moments at a time.
The students' feet dangle, awkward,
then try to meet the ground—suddenly there
as it's always there. Even such brief
joinings with air, with absence,
must give them a sense that the world
can be left behind, that one can choose
the landscape of the mind. I imagine
their goal, small brushes with death
made beautiful, the spirit drifting off
where it will.

We take a picnic to the woods above them,
noticing, as we climb, the hawks'
continuing patterns, with and against
the wind. They are a kind of silent music,
notes on the blue, a rhythm that repeats,
slow loops I'd say were nocturnes
if this were night, and the long glissandos
of dives.

We find a spot in the trees where flakes
of light filter through, and then a whole
patch of it, bright, where the wind
doesn't enter. I think of snow, how Wisconsin
this time of year can already be glazed
with a white that mutes sound and difference.
Higher, where the Pyrenees define Andorre,
that may have begun. But here
in the foothills, we shed our jeans,

make love on the old blue bedspread
we keep in the car. Sun spills
into my eyes, a blinding that makes pines
disappear in a golden blaze, and we too
float on the quick heat that could be
midsummer. When shadows begin to darken
the grass, our skin wants clothes again.
We drive to the highest ridge
where we can see a line of overlapping peaks
stretch hazily to Spain. We leave
before they disappear with the day.
Halfway back, the hawks still circle
toward dusk, a falling melody, the year
easing down.

IN A DIFFICULT KEY

For Paul Martin

In the years when love
was the jargoning of orioles,
you danced the oberek, your legs
flying out like spokes as you wheeled
across the living room,
your body's coin spun
on its thin brilliance.
Your famous muscles were as tuned
as the polished piano
that was half your world.
Then health was a simple assumption
everyone made, and when you gimbled,
marching to the dining room,
it was just the show.

Now you've entered a sober country
where you must perform the egg dance,
blindfold fastened, your nimble feet
gone numb, so that to step
is to stumble. Each crushed egg
might be a month, might be a year.
We who love you would be alchemists,
turning those eggs to gold.
You would gambol among them, among us,
your awkward audience, decades
before growing old.

ROSES

For Tony Kish

You descend like a monk
to the chapel in the castle's
depths, where you close
yourself in. Your cowl
of Cluny lace shadows your face
in patterns of wheat
and wagon wheels, the fields
of your ancestors printed there,
almost waving. You see
that the rose window
has been sealed with cement.
You lock the door, the irremeable
stone stairs behind it,
and think of that window—
how hard it would be to knock
the cement from the frame. And what
would be left? Fragments
of Rose Plum, bluer and paler
than Tourmaline Pink or Daphne?
Not quite the Rose of Heaven
that purples your skin
in clusters like grapes.
You grin, appreciate
such ironies, then sing another name—
Rose of Jericho, the resurrection plant.
You sit on a cold bench, dry,
your knees to your chin.

Then the tide begins to rise
in the ruined chapel
where a river runs through,
papyrus columns springing up
along the soft banks
of my dream, the only thing
I have to give you.

NEW ORLEANS FEATHER SCULPTOR
DIES OF KNIFE WOUNDS

Blood fans on the waxed parquet
like feathers, like the cape I made
for Neil, plumes
that spread, scarlet peacock's tail,
when he whirled. He leapt
through the air to fall on its circular
softness, all grace, his long
lean body curled to its fiery
circumference.

Now I lie here, no dancer's mime
but the real death coming,
and I do not feel fear. We all
know worse ways to die.

I drift into dreams of Mick Jagger,
who wore my headdress,
once took it all over the country,
fringes, fingers of blue
fanning his brow when
he bowed, his fine
azure eyes beneath them
catching the color.

Maybe it wasn't a knife,
but a sharp blue quill,
the extension of someone's
lonely hand, some man who yearned
for brilliance, who coveted
my kind of beauty.

THE VISITATION

All the princes were changing,
their golden locks falling out,
silken bodies thinning
to lines and angles,
the geometry of loss. You,
my friend, had spiked your hair
and turned it an intentional gray.
Bound for California, you swore,
as danger blinked its hot
white lights and you closed
your eyes. Then a glass
shattered in someone's hand,
blood spilling from his fingers
like spells. I am the fable
for our time, he cried,
baring his teeth. We are all
each other's nightmares—
our faces, spun like coins,
flash the nether side of love.

GABRIEL'S STORY

Riverhead, NY—A minister charged with sexually abusing three
girls and a boy while pretending to be the angel Gabriel was
convicted of statutory rape and other charges.

Each incarnation takes faith, but patience
is rewarded, always. When Hilda died,
I became the widower the neighbors saw,
his head perpetually bowed, his hands shaking
like the drunkards' he saved over and over,
until their sins passed through him, evaporated,
leaving only the smallest residue in his soul.

In the mirror, skin grayer each day, I saw
I couldn't keep my pale right eye from twitching.
Women brought cakes and casseroles and pots
of beans until the freezer wouldn't hold them.
Only when I crawled under Hilda's wedding quilt
did I begin to trust God's plan.
I stayed there weeks, the Martha Circle coming
to change the sheets, to feed me broth
with a spoon. One of them spoke
in my mother's voice, another, at last,
in God's. She told me to fast seven days,
to refuse the soup and to stay as I was,
knees to my chin in the darkened room.
When at the end of that time I threw
the curtains back, sun would break through
the glass like revelation, and I'd know
who I'd become.

It happened. A Monday morning
but the light wasn't as she'd promised.
No, a rainy dawn when I rose
and shook out damp wings. I stood there
in the sweaty air, raised
the window, and felt clouds enter,
the whole room turn to steam.
I rose on it, weightless,
as if my body had disappeared,
except that the wings
began to fan, and oddly, as they dried,
grew heavier. All that day
I wandered through the house

learning how not to bruise them
on door frames, how to fold them
so close they'd scarcely brush my legs.

When I went out to the park near dusk,
two women cheered. I didn't recognize them,
hurried past them toward the gardens
where Hilda and I used to pray.
Love of my loins, are you truly gone?
I heard myself say toward the trees.
And then someone came as a child
out from the roses, and I saw
it was Hilda. I wrapped her in my wings,
her small mouth pouting
the way she always did when I took her
from what she was stirring in the kitchen,
wrestled her to our bed. The rustling
of her dress was the sound
of my heart flying,
her cries a sure and passionate blessing,
the music of the spheres.

REHEARSALS

After Henri Rousseau's *The Sleeping Gypsy*

Surely the lion, that curious cat,
has no malicious intentions.
He sniffs around the sleeping man
the way he'd put his nose to a flower.
Exploratory. Not imagination
(the guitar) about to be devoured.
Too easy. The man's dreams
are becoming nightmares,
that part's true. He feels
the hot breath on his back,
perhaps even smells stale blood.
But we who have troubled sleep
know how many lions can prowl
through a single night, the ruffs
on their necks tickling,
half-rousing us, then
letting us slide
toward what we hope will be rest.
The gypsy has chosen the open air,
a comfortable dune, the full moon
that whitens his already
luminous robe. The music he hears
is the music he makes. When
he dreams danger, that too
is his own devising. Aren't there lions
who slink through his days,
who have to be slain?
This playing possum is practice.
Soon he'll strut like a hero,
a man who has walked
into the world's rapacious mouth
and out, awake, alive.

THE PAL LUNCH

After Edward Hopper's *Nighthawks*, 1942

The year of my birth, my father's cafe.
But it's not my father behind the counter
bending to look for matches, a lock
of blond hair falling over his forehead
like a thought he brushes away. He stuffs
that hair back under the creased
white hat shaped like the soldiers' caps
they must all have worn, those short-order cooks
who were also the waiters, the owners.
He's commenting on the empty stools,
how he likes this hour, when people
are few, when most have drifted away,
their hands in their pockets.

No, my father's the one in the gray fedora,
my mother's beside him. In a reversal
like dream, they're the customers, leaning
easily on elbows, heavy white coffee mugs
steaming before them. He's just asked
for a light. He'd tried to strike up
a conversation with the man whose back
is to us, but no dice. That man is tired,
a little drunk. So the one behind the counter
and my father talk of the war, the draft.
They can't know the blond man will die in France
or that my father survives the Pacific.
My mother nods, her hands still slim,
white and delicate-veined as the peonies
she grows. This is long before arthritis
takes root in her fingers.
Huge coffee machines gleam silver
beside them, under fluorescent bulbs,
one buzzing off and on like a faint alarm.

They are not lonely, there in the bright cafe,
while darkness inhabits the street outside
where no cars are, neither parked nor moving.
They relax, for once the ones who sit, leisure
resting lightly on their shoulders.
They can go home and to bed whenever
they wish, to the house on Reuter Avenue,

the bedroom of soft chenille
and the oval mirror low enough
for a child, later, to see
her whole self in their image.
They will not have to rise before dawn
to come here, to heat the polished grill
and mix the pancake batter.

My father lights his fifth cigarette
in an hour. The smoke obscures their faces,
a cloud that passes over them quick as years.
My mother goes to the rest room,
puts on fresh lipstick, rearranges her hair.

My grandmother waits at home with me,
checking her watch, wondering
what could possess them,
where in the world they might be.

THE DIFFICULT LIFE OF IDEAS

The limp toward the horizon hardly hearing
the birds cawing, calling—voices that skip
toward noon. They are concentrating,
they want to perfect themselves. There is longing
in their silence, their awkwardness,
but they cannot bring breath into themselves
by will. Rabbits skitter across the hills,
escaping guns. Chestnuts fall.
Farmers rumble by on tractors.
There's real pain in the walk uphill,
the sun's grown stronger. They stop to rest,
spirits diminishing in the heat. Now they wish
only for arrival, a house where they can lie down,
someone to feed them quail and plums.

POEM TO THE IDEAL READER

You are the twin my mother
gave away at birth,
suddenly arrived from out west,
Arizona, where you grew up
with horses and novels and Prokofiev,
your foster parents musicians.
While I thought you'd died,
you were listening to violin concertos
and training colts, waiting
for the day I'd flee the snow
and head for a land
of perpetual blossoms. (Even now,
as winter deepens, red and white camellias
bloom out the bedroom window.)
While you studied desert owls
and words, I ranged innocent
and lonely through the world—
to Spain and France and Italy,
to the sad Balkans. Now you are here,
your old Volkswagen piled to its ceiling,
the whole backseat, with books.
I take you for walks on the beach,
where we stop to watch porpoises—
new to us both—our hair tangling
in the wind. Whatever
lines I suggest, you nod,
your face telling me gently
yes or no. I sleep
so much better, you
in the next room, up reading
all night with candles.

WATCHING MYSELF COMPOSE

Only Peterson's shoe store had one—
a mahogany box you could stand against,
feet thrust into a space
where the x-ray promised and gave
a webbed vision,
thin bones gleaming green,
iridescent through the viewer.

I stretched my young spine to reach it,
to bend to the window,
the mystery revealed
like something forbidden,
its eerie image taking me back
somewhere before my own birth.

It was like seeing into the heart
of your life, when you
can nearly remember
the first steps you took,
how one trembling foot
went ahead of the other
and you were free, or could see
freedom coming, your own
legs taking you far, oh far
from home.

Whenever we passed that store,
I ran in to look: there was a way
to see growth, to see how to fit
outside to inside,
how to watch the self
compose over years

while the rays must have drifted
out through the room
where farmers sat
with their scraped-off boots
beside them, and young women
waited, their curls sleeked down
into hairpinned rolls
framing earnest faces,
some with babies beginning
inside them, each of them
smiling, each waiting
his turn, her turn.

WHAT IF

when you entered your mind
with purpose, you found not the field
you'd told yourself to imagine, the wild
strawberries of childhood strewn
among the tall grass where you lay
under apple trees, but a land flatter
and wider than sight could take in.
What if you forgot how to bring inside
the music that used to begin
in your gradual wakings, and in the space
before sleep, when rain began softly,
and all your sweet longings loosened.
What if traffic and telephones
continued their commerce, so loud
you couldn't remember how your skin felt,
floating. There is this fear
stalking the hours. One day
it might disappear, that place
you could go at will, where your own
voice hummed like a mother,
a crooning that let your blood
slow, the poem of the body
riding blue murmuring crests, naming
its love, loving its life.

DREAMING ANOTHER VERSION

The sheep, asleep in their bays,
will not move when I yell
that it's storming, they must
get to the barn. A cockatoo,
white as the first breast,
tries to bite. Three yellow
cockatiels follow me out
of their cage, sail
into the garden, where animals
swarm and swim, dark
in the goldfish bowl.
I am their mother, then mother
to dozens of children, their eyes
misted. They run from the rain
into shelters. I button sweaters
around them, brown and red sweaters,
spinning from one to another,
their silver cheeks streaked
in the lightning's glow,
their faces one face
in the moon's sudden mirror.

JASMINE

Phan Thi Kim Phuc, now 22, travels throughout the U.S. giving
speeches, raising money for plastic surgery to repair her scars.

Think of how you saw her first:
naked, nine, screaming,
her napalmed arms lifted
like wings that would not
rise. No relief, no matter
how far, how fast she fled
or imagined flying. Burns
on her back, her chest,
drilled in, spread out,
so that she thought
she was dying,
would disappear in one
of the agonized rushes
that licked off her skin.
We remember her mouth,
a dark moon of grief.

Nights she dreams
of fire drifting down,
her body a flower
whose petals curl and grow black
before they're quite open.

She feels herself
buried alive, her skin
peeling off in sheets
so that before sleep comes
she's already bones.

But clouds overhead now are only
clouds. In storms
rain is cool, sweet
water, like rivers
she swims in.

"Forgiveness,"
she tells the press,
is her body's reason
to travel a country
where some men remember
children exploding

in the air
beneath them,
fragments of flesh
floating down
from the sky.

Beauty rises up and says
to the beast,
"The war is over,
the past is the past."

The beast has been prowling
a long time now. He can
hardly hear that voice,
a lute in his ear.

Can scarcely see
through the shaggy hair
covering his eyes
the lilies blooming
before him.
But the scent—the scent
of jasmine on the air
begins to reach him.

How to be the forgiven?
All the grace
is in her.

May our scars lighten
to white, as they do
over years. Let each one
be a blossom, pure
as original pain
transformed, yet itself,
so that we cannot forget
what was there.

A lovely young woman leans
into the camera, hair falling
over her carefully
camouflaged shoulders.
As palm leaves fan
behind, we strain
to imagine the air
become jasmine.

IT BEGINS WITH A PRESENTIMENT

The way, when I was ill,
exhaustion came over me so fast
I knew I had to find a bed,
then fell instantly to sleep.
This is not sleep but something
closer to trance,
the scratch of pen on paper
already part of the music
that's coming, not in tune—
that shifts, the way a dream
slides, you're going right
when you could have sworn
the old farmhouse was to the left,
where dust kicked up by a palomino
still floats down,
forming a wreath around
a young girl's head.
All you can do is follow,
meandering through the black-eyed
Susan ditch, humming the theme
from a movie. You will discover
a barn where kittens drop
from their mother when you pick her up,
wet notes so small you have to magnify
the sound to hear it, to keep hearing it
for years. Where are you going?
You didn't know then,
though paradise was palpable
and lines of cedar
sheltered the path out.
Now you have a better idea
where it will end. But the going
remains fragrant, the blood
unaware of age, wild in its autumn heart
even as it notices, then counts
irregular beats.

THIS ORDINARY WALTZ

For most of us, grace is not natural,
it has to be learned.
There's always someone
rearranging your rooms, so that when
you come home late and try not to wake
the house, every step is a trial
and each fall repeats old layers
of bruises. If you should manage
the second floor landing
with the spindly chairs, it's
potentially fatal. I knew a frail man
whose wife didn't wait for accidents,
who pushed him so that he fell
down the stairs, his neck
broken like the stem of a lily.
His son could not prove intent
but knew, though in truth
there is just as often no malice,
what happens happens. The music
shifts tempo, you're dancing
double-time, and the heart leaps
as in love, then falters.
You find yourself in a white room,
the sun rising and setting
so fast you think it's a film
speeded up, your only window
brilliantly blank, then black,
the dawn in between a quick hint
of pink before the day
rolls blindingly in again.

MONDE RENVERSÉ

Negative: the left good side of your face
become the right, your characteristic
gesture, hand describing an arc,
caught midway through,
moves counterclockwise
emphasizing an opposite point.
At first everything seems
as normal as any Sunday, but then
we feel something amiss,
the eyebrow that usually droops
lifted like a tic.
An uncomfortable moment, seeing
not ourselves but the selves
someone might impersonate,
Duchamp as Rrose Selavy, features
disguised by a pen's
drawn curls, what's
shadow now prominent
as cheekbones, something closer
to how we'll emerge after death,
androgynous skulls
mocking who we were.

CONTAINING THE LIGHT

Yet I wonder if an image of the imagination is ever close to
reality.

—Gaston Bachelard

    Disappearance is the fear—
    not of the self, which can drone on
    like November wind in Wisconsin,
    on into December, through March,
    even April, the ceaseless wind that sings
    ghost songs through windows as tight
    as a grandfather's carpenter hands
    could make them. Between green swirls
    of plaster and oak frames,
    it varies its dissonant pitch,
    but not the lament. No,
    it's the past leaking out that keeps us
    awake all night, keeps us making corrections.

    Today the leaves are falling faster
    than I can sweep them
    from the patio. The sun is almost warm
    on my back, the garden's colors deepen,
    and old Octobers offer themselves.
    What can be resurrected?
    The way the light did not shatter
    but bent our shadows against
    sixth century walls in Dubrovnik,
    against cool stone, against
    the promises of centuries, soon again
    to be broken? Or how, the year
    we married, the soft air of the village
    was much like here in Carolina.
    What blurs is how love takes
    the fading light and turns it gold,
    keeps turning it, in and out of itself,
    while what burns burns deeper.

    I think of a lonely road where pears
    ripen, never quite sweetly,
    and how it becomes the path
    to a hill where a castle fallen to ruin
    is partially rebuilt, then left
    to itself again, blackberries thickening

the way back down to where the Virgin
reveals herself white as bone
as the trees begin to lose their amplitude.
Where do they rest, the falls
that gave us ourselves and led us here?
Their shapes grow skeletal,
the light paler, even as beauty
thins, pared to essentials.

SFUMATO

How nothing leads to everything—
the canvas more densely white
than a blizzard, a womb so blank
even intention would get lost there.
But of course this is wrong.
The beginning is the place itself,
and then something, some things
coming together, the way pollen sifts
through late summer, charming
next year's colors into being.
Light angles in through a window
making a shadow that can be traced
with a brush or a pencil, the shading
followed until form emerges, a figure
of a man or a woman, a man and a woman,
their genesis something else, embryos
we recognize or don't, the way
a dream will bring one to the surface,
the child suddenly woman caught
between allegiances, so that she does not
see the room you made, but walks past
and says with her walk
how much distance she must keep.
We weave our way through,
the warp thread twisted
so that later, faint stripes
will catch the sun. Sometimes
even pain inches toward celebration,
shades lightening again,
nothing fixed, nothing like a woman
loved because she never changes, but how
we move more softly through our worlds.

VISITING EINSTEIN IN
WASHINGTON, D.C.

Snow covers the pages
of his stone book
but his eyes aren't focused
there. The world
goes on, inside
and out, particles drifting
through light the way snow
organizes the sky—sometimes
vertically, chalk lines
dividing what we can barely see.
Sometimes one would have to stand
farther back than any window,
watch from the caboose of a train
racing into space
to find a pattern, time
run backward to when snow
drifted to the low bare
branches of maples, to the sills,
and at the driveway's edge mounded
so high it blotted out the sun.
Turn a corner and the earth tilts.
In Carolina, it comes,
but like an angel, welcomed
for infrequent good news,
his way of making everyone believe
that change is possible—
not only possible, but nearly
instantaneous, the way the mind
makes beauty, and lets it go.

LASTING

When the first radio wave music escaped Earth's ionosphere, it
literally did become eternal. Music, in this century, has been
converted from sound into the clarity of pure light. Radio has
superseded the constraints of space.

—Leonard Shlain, *Art & Physics*

Imagine Vivaldi suddenly falling
on the ears of a woman
somewhere beyond Alpha Centauri,
her planet spun into luminescence
aeons from now. She might be
much like us, meditating
on the body, her lover murmuring
to the underside of her breast
before its heaviness suspends,
for a moment, the lift and pause
of his breath. A music she almost knows
drifts through centuries, startling,
augmenting her pleasure.
When earth is particles of dust,
Orson Welles may still strike fear
into the hearts of millions
who wake one morning, unaware
that light has arrived
as an audible prank. Ezra Pound might rasp
his particular madness from an Italy
still alive in arias that shower
into the open windows
of a world youthful as hope.
When books are no longer even ashes,
and no heart beats in any space
near where we were, suns
may intersect, and some of our voices
blend into choirs, the music of the spheres
adrift among new stars.